Hidden in the jungle

Peggy Nille

A Search and Find Book

PETER PAUPER PRESS, INC.
White Plains, New York

T0019594

Search and Find

ALL 20 CREATURES
IN EVERY SCENE:

A lazy leopard

A super peacock

A baby giraffe and his father

A vibrant butterfly

A curious lizard

A slithering snake

A silly rhinoceros

Two flamingos in love

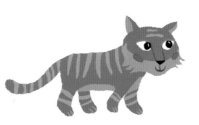

A baby tiger

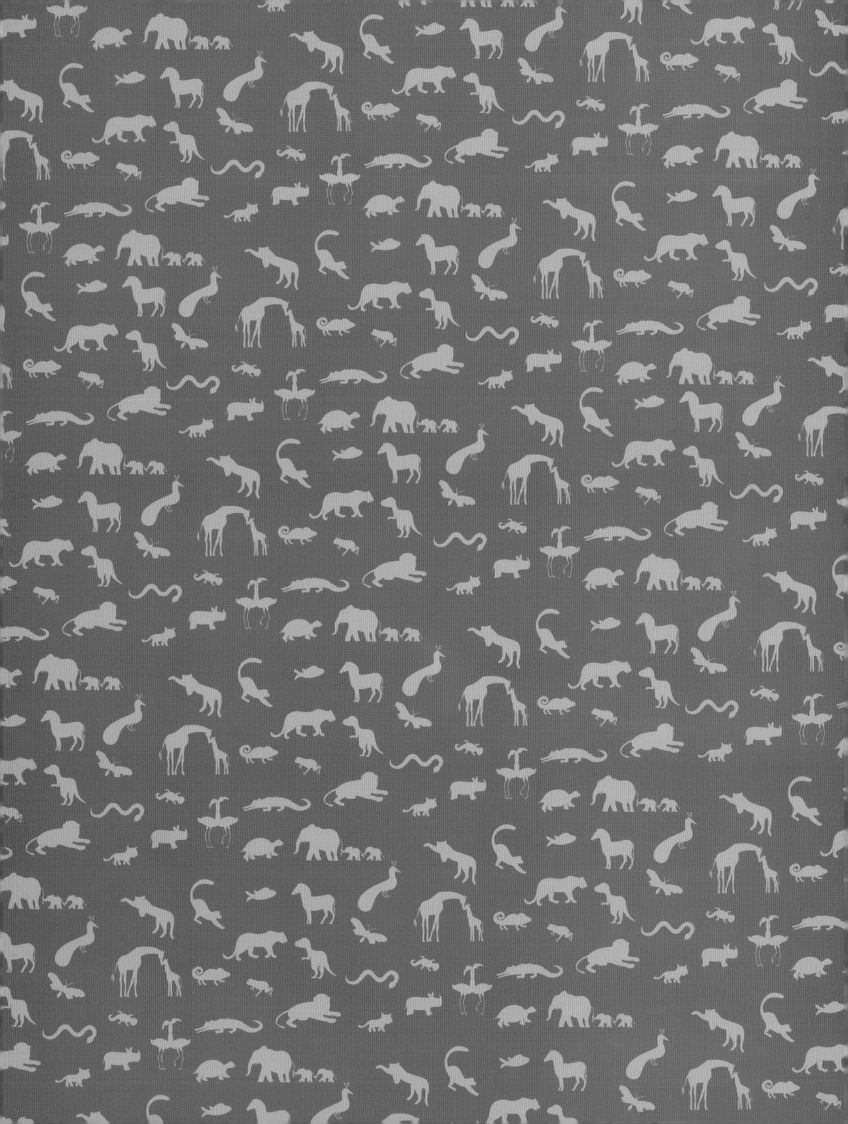

PETER PAUPER PRESS
Fine Books and Gifts Since 1928

Our Company

In 1928, at the age of twenty-two, Peter Beilenson began printing books on a small press in the basement of his parents' home in Larchmont, New York. Peter—and later, his wife, Edna—sought to create fine books that sold at "prices even a pauper could afford."

Today, still family owned and operated, Peter Pauper Press continues to honor our founders' legacy of quality, value, and fun for big kids and small kids alike.

To Rousseau, "Le Douanier"

First published in France under the title *Cachés dans la jungle* © Actes Sud, Paris, 2017
Original edits by François Martin assisted by Marine Tasso; Art direction and design originally done by Kamy Pakdel and Christelle Grossin.

First published in the USA in 2018 by Peter Pauper Press, Inc.
English edition copyright © 2018 by Peter Pauper Press, Inc.

Published by Peter Pauper Press, Inc.
202 Mamaroneck Avenue
White Plains, New York 10601 USA

Library of Congress Cataloging-in-Publication Data Available

ISBN 978-1-4413-2653-9
Manufactured for Peter Pauper Press, Inc.
Printed in China

7 6 5 4
Visit us at www.peterpauper.com

A long-tailed lemur

A flying fish

A green and blue zebra

A prancing panther

A friendly dinosaur

A colorful chameleon

A spotted frog

A regal lion

A sly alligator

A slow and steady turtle

A mama elephant and her twins

SOLUTIONS

1.

2.

3.

4.

5.

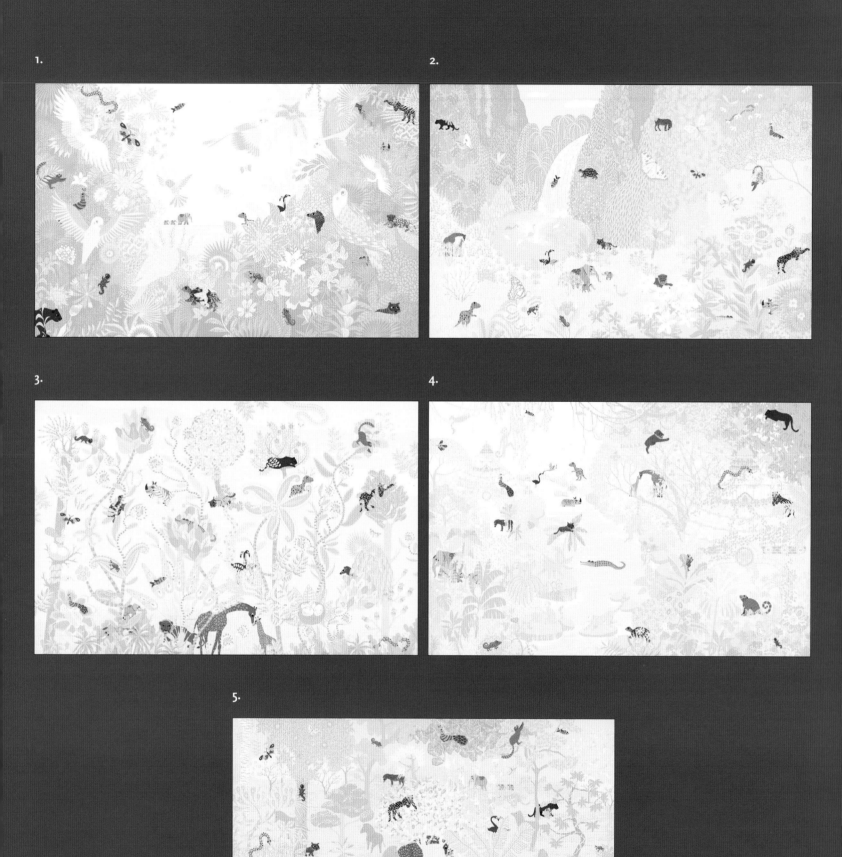

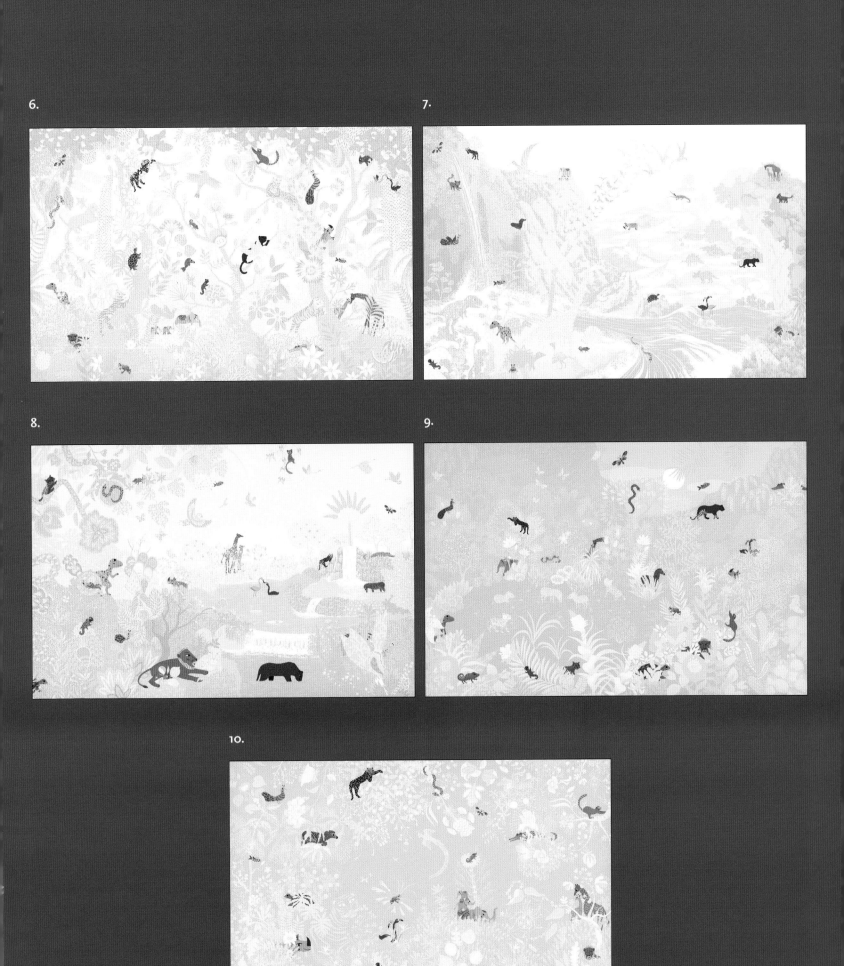

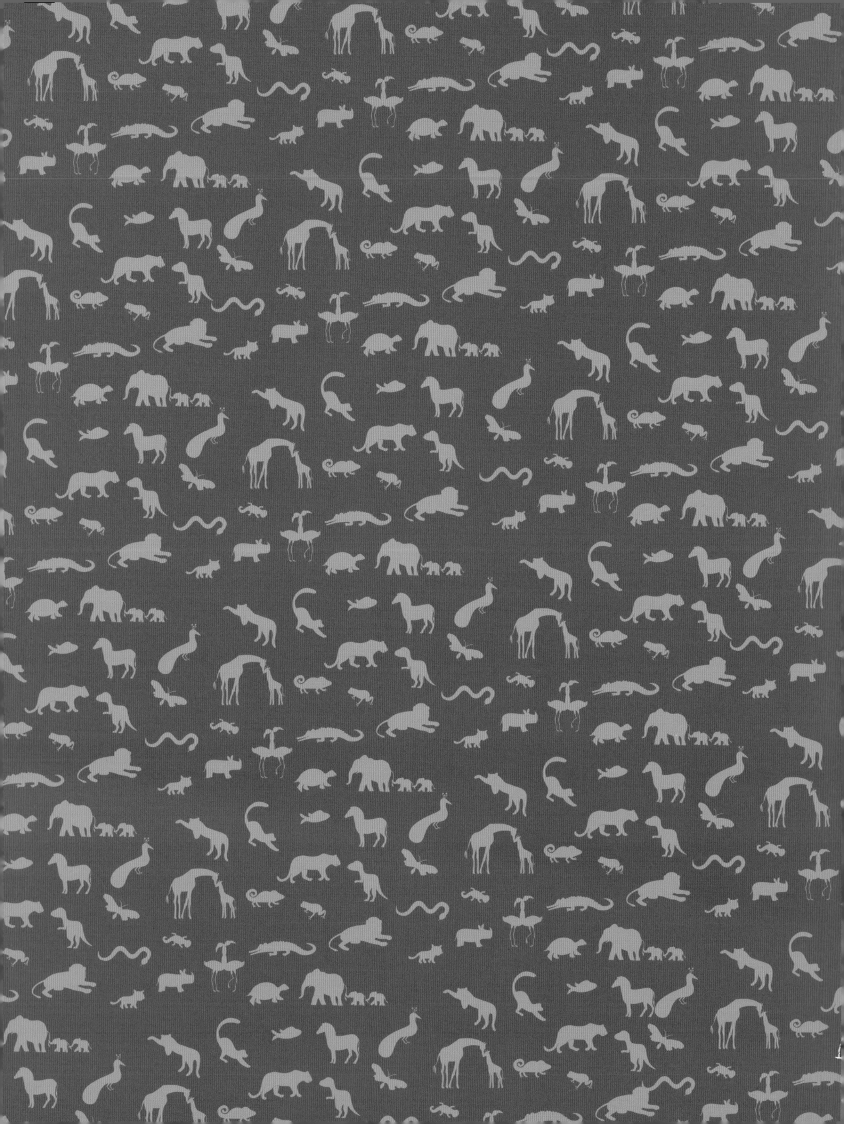